AF408184

The Weed

Halley Tiefert

I wake in my niece's bedroom
Emotionally barren
I go to the kitchen and reach into the cabinet
And pull out a white mug with a blue interior
And sprays and bouquets of flowers rounding the rim
I know this mug.
I found it at a thrift store 10 years ago for my first college apartment
Where me and my friends sipped coffee and wine spritzers
From any vessel we could find
It came home with me after graduation
Where my mom and I used it
A cup of decaf with a slice of cheesecake at night
I must've left it there when I left my hometown
And I forgot my favorite little mug in the excitement of change
Soon, my sister visited our parents –
On her way out the door for her long drive home,
My mother handed her a cup of coffee
So the mug lived with her for a while.
Until she brought it in with some things
When she visited our sister in law.
So here it is now, back in my hand
Standing in my brother's kitchen
In the home his wife has opened to me.
I stir cream into my coffee
My life is new today.
And here's this little mug
Reflecting the way we can weave in and out of each other's lives
A sweet reminder of the way we quietly love each other

Love bears all things
So I was his nurse
taking his temperature
and smoothing his hair back
I will bear the weight of your illness

Love believes all things
So I believed
If I love him enough
Treat him with kindness
He will return it one day

Love endures all things
So I waited for him to stop yelling
I apologized
I was being a cunt
I begged his forgiveness

Better to live in a desert than with a quarrelsome and nagging wife
So he was right and I was sorry
And I will submit to my husband
And god, why can't I be better
I have to give respect to receive it

In humility value others above yourselves
So I did my best to meet his needs
And prayed for God to change my heart
So I could do it without resentment
For all my own sacrifices

All have sinned and fallen short of the glory of God
So I was no better than he
Because all sin is equal in His eyes
So it wasn't fair to focus on his sins
And forgive my own

Love, joy, peace, patience, kindness, goodness, faithfulness, gentleness, self control
Check, miss, miss, miss, miss, miss, miss, miss, miss
Bad Christian, bad wife, bad woman

I promised in front of god to take him
For better; for worse
For richer; for poorer
In sickness and in health
Til death do us part

So now I'm a liar, a vow-breaker
Prayer should have helped
Forgiveness should have helped
Love was supposed to fix it

Love does not have to endure all things

The circus tent
The spotlight is on the circus tent when you go at night
To see the clowns and trapeze artists and elephants
The circus tent screams,
"Look at me! Come see! We'll have so much fun!"
Under that spotlight, the tent shines bright red,
Like the candy apple you can't wait to sink your teeth into.
Lights flash, music blares,
Welcoming you to come look, laugh, see the spectacle!

That night the exhausted carnies pack up the tent
And move to the next city.
If you went to see them set it up in the morning,
You'd see the frayed edges escaping hems.
You'd see that the candy apple red is really sun-damaged, dull orange.

Maybe later you'd think back and be able to see more cracks.
You'd remember how the rides creaked and groaned with weight,
The cruelty that put the elephants inside that tent,
The broken tooth caused by the candy apple.
You'd think,
"It was fun, but I wouldn't go again."
You've experienced all the circus has to offer,
And found it lacking.

Years after that, the circus will come to town again.
You'll say,
"Oh, I went years ago, but I don't remember much about it."
You wouldn't even be able to remember what color the tent was
If someone asked.
You'll tell the story of the dentist
Who smelled like stale cigarettes
And fixed the tooth you broke on the candy apple
And you won't even think of the tent and its phony brightness again.

Don't look too long
Don't stay past closing.
When the bartenders start doing that line about not going home,
Go home.

I'm not a sparkler burning out,
Not a piece of silver tarnishing with time.
I'm worse–
Sparkling in the light,
But the longer you look,
The duller my shine.

A disco ball
Just held together by disintegrating glue
Missing so many mirrors,
The dull black plastic showing through.

A shot of cheap tequila
A little too warm
To be enjoyed on a dark dance floor
And forgotten in the morning.

In the daylight, you'll see the chips in my finish.
I'm funnier with the music up,
Prettier with my clothes off.
Fun for a moment, but not for an hour.

So go home while I'm still interesting
While I'm still a prism
Reflecting rainbows in your eyes.
You won't remember the girl who laughed so loudly
And pulled you in so close
But pushed you into the car
And waved goodbye at the end of the night

You'll never know that I saved you.
You'll never know how much you would resent me in time,
How bored you'd be in a few months.
You won't know how trapped you'd feel if you stayed,
Or the guilt that would build inside you as you became unkind.
You'll never know the rage you would've felt coming home to see me.
You'll never know how violently you would wish you could shake me
        with every "I'm sorry."
How much you would want to strangle the words "I love you" from my throat.
You will never dream of cracking my head on the counter top
To watch all my selfless love splatter like brain matter on the tile.
Or of watching my liquid longing pouring out,
        pooling at the bottom of the stairs.
You'll never have to bury my love letters in a shallow grave under your bed.
Or scatter the ashes of us at our favorite beach in South Carolina
You'll never know the fate I had to save you from–
You'll never know me,
You'll never love me,
So you'll never hate me.

I am working on my house.
It's a whole renovation,
I'm tearing down walls,
Replacing tiles,
Refinishing the hardwood,
Building new furniture.
And it's hard.
It takes extra work–
Is this a load-bearing wall?
I have to sand this before painting.
Ripping up the carpet to get to the floor.
I wonder if it would be easier
To do this from the ground up.
I wish you'd just burnt my house down.

Alexis

I hope someone will drive hours to wander aimlessly
(while they have pneumonia)
To listen to your hurts,
So you can see yourself reflected in their eyes
While they cry for your broken heart
So you can know what kind of love you deserve.

I hope someone will carry your heart like it's fragile
Without fear of dropping it
Because they know it so well
The slipperiest places and the strongest footholds
So they can hold it firm and steady.

I hope someone will call you first with their very best news
So you can share their joy
Because they know you will feel it with them
They know you will tell them they deserve it
And actually believe it.

I hope you will feel the incredible lightness
That comes with love sans expectations.
I hope you find out that nothing is better
Than being deemed insufferable by everyone
(other than yourself and the love of your life)
Because you can't breathe around your laughter
When it bubbles around you like a champagne bath.
I hope you get to experience the euphoria
Of knowing someone loves you as much as you love them.

I'm not mad at God, I just don't hear from him anymore. No, nothing happened, we just kinda drifted apart. After my breakup, we were both just so busy, I didn't hear from Him much and I wasn't really reaching out either and then we just were like, in different circles. No, we didn't fight or anything, there wasn't an event, we just drifted after that. I mean, there were a bunch of people around Him that I didn't really like but that's not really on Him. I will always have love for God, He was there for me through SO much, for my whole life. No, I've literally known Him since before I was born. He genuinely saved my life. Like more than once. We're just not really close anymore. Have you spoken to Him recently? Oh nice, how is He? Good, good. I love to hear that. Yeah, He doesn't have social media so I can't even keep up with Him that way. It's so good to hear y'all are still so close. Like I just want all good things for Him. And for you, obviously. If you see Him, make sure you tell Him hi for me. Ohmigod but, tell me about that guy you hooked up with last week, you said he was into clown stuff?

There is no archetype for you
No stock character,
No box to put you in.
If you were a villain it'd be easier
A storybook nemesis
An illustrated classic
Drawn with a permanent scowl
Followed by a cloud of smoke
I can hate a villain
They despise the pure of heart
Longing for the pain of the hero
Motivated only by their downfall
If you were only here to antagonize me
To jumpstart the plot of my life
To hurt me as a means to an end
That would make sense
If that were the case
I would gain my wings
And kiss the prince
And leave you behind without a thought
...
But I know about what you like
And the things that make you laugh
I have seen your tears
I know your hurts
You're not an archetype
I'm not a heroine
We don't have sidekicks or henchmen
There won't be a showdown
If there is a villain it's me
For knowing your hurts
And still adding to them
Because I didn't want to hurt
I am not pure of heart
I am the selfish sinner
Who can't love you anymore
And can't hate you either

Every day I remind the universe that I want to go first.
I wish for a car crash,
Or a break-in gone wrong,
Or a piano falling from the sky.
Something with a big settlement left for you
To make missing me easier

If I went first you'd be propped up.
But too many others would miss you with me.
Seeing your face in the mirror
I would crumble like a picked flower after too much sun
Disintegrate like a paper grocery bag in a hurricane

I don't want you to hurt
It's not right to choose your pain over mine
Your goodness contrasted by my selfishness
It's proof you should be the one to stay.

Me without you is Earth without sun.
Your warmth and kindness feeding the greenery
That couldn't grow in the cold

I promise I won't leave before my time
I won't make any moves to hurt you

But I will pray that my time comes first until it's here.

Glimmers from a Corporate Girl Weekday

The chirp of a small, warm kitty cat before I turn my lamp on. The glide of the french press. The swirl of the cream in my coffee and the delicate china cup I sip from. The way everything in my lunch box stacks together just so. The fresh outside air on the walk to the car. The pinky glow on the horizon as the sun comes up. Getting the best parking space because it's early. The thick click of the switch on the coffee maker. Watching coworkers entering in varied states of readiness for the day – some cheerful and bright, others shuffling, bleary-eyed, some waving silently, others calling out or smiling or even coming by to chat. The pride of being recognized. Sitting by a sunny window for lunch break. Small talk and gossip with coworkers. The sweetness in the mug of mint tea at 2 PM. That rich coffee aroma filling the air as the machine grinds the beans for tomorrow's coffee. The sun kissing my face on the drive home. The freedom feeling when no one else is in the gym. The warmth of the shower and the slide of soap on my skin. The slip of my hair as I work it through the brush and blow dryer. The silky satin of my pillowcase.

I walk through the backgrounds of other peoples' lives
Specifically designed to be unremarkable.
Not to be despised, not to be adored.
If I'm lucky I provide support to the heroes and main characters.
Here's a pair of extra special shoes
Here's a loaf of bread
Here's some intel on the villain
Otherwise I'm just noise–
A piece of gossip in a bar
A seductive word in a brothel
A sob echoing through a pillaged town
(my best work).
I'm a fully realized character,
With a background, and emotions, and reactions programmed in
Drifting with the wind
To bolster everyone else's purpose
And have none of my own

You didn't love me for me
You loved me despite me

Not loved for my warm soft heart–
Loved even though I was too sensitive

Not loved for being silly–
Loved even though I'm annoying

Not loved for my openness–
Loved even though I talk too much

Not loved for my determination–
Loved even though I'm delusional

Loved not for who I am-
Loved despite not being who I'm supposed to be

And despised for wanting more

The Dress

There's this dress
THE Dress
It's supposed to be universally flattering,
To even unlock your True Potential.
It's wildly expensive,
You'll pay for it the rest of your life,
But you can't even unlock your femininity without it,
You won't even know what it's really like to be a woman
Until you have The Dress.
You won't know true love
Until you have The Dress.
"What if it doesn't look good on me?" I ask
"Nonsense," they say, "we are Made to wear The Dress.
It's flattering on everyone."
But I've tried on The Dress
I've tried it on in department stores and boutiques.
I've tried on my sister's Dress, my best friend's–
And I don't like it on me.
The Dress exhausts me.
It makes me angry, squeezing me in all the wrong ways until I can't breathe.
"No, no," they say, "it's different when it's your own Dress."
And I look around at the women I know
Who have The Dress
They glow, they shine with joy in being A Dress Owner
And I wonder about the women like me
Who don't want to sacrifice for The Dress
The women who know they would resent The Dress if they had it
What do we do to feel complete the way they do?
Were they already complete and The Dress just changed them
So they feel More because they're Different?

Laughter is the shiny armor protecting me from every barb of my memories
Alcohol slurs the speech of my inner critic
I let go of the insecurities that beget themselves over and over,
Dancing in the dark, glitter on my eyes
Cigarette smoke clings to my sticky skin
And I chase that feeling
Freedom and blooming confidence
My hips sway and I am suddenly Aphrodite,
I am beautiful, girls, we are so beautiful
The most beautiful girls in the world are here in this bar
So no
I don't want to heal
It's easier to be angry
It's more fun to be fucked up
I won't be a clamshell lacquering beautiful, soft layers on the surface of a pearl
I will hold onto all the hurt,
Squeezing and squashing it
Until a sparkling diamond emerges
Cold and hard
Desirable and untouchable

What happens when I have no more sordid details to share?

When all of my stories run dry, run stale?

I have this awful, sinking feeling that everyone will find the truth:

The secret that I try to keep even from myself:

Mild
Gentle
Meek
Weak
All words used to describe me
I only ever felt small, vulnerable
There was nothing meek about the primal sounds
    that escaped me on the worst nights
I wonder if he will remember a ferocity in my eye while I begged him to hurt me
The way I remember poison on his tongue
That bit through my thin shirt, soaking through my skin,
    absorbing into my bloodstream

"You rock the natural look," my friend tells me.
And all I can think about is someone else asking me
When I was going to start wearing makeup again.
Another friend squeezes me at the end of a long lunch date and says,
"I just love spending time with you,"
And His voice echoes in my ear,
"I've been trying to get away from you for years."
My sister peals in laughter as we create another silly character
And still He is there, whispering,
"You're not fun."
In a world of laughter and sunshine and time
And people who love me
He is somehow ever present,
Exposing all of my weak points:
I am tormenting the ones I love most,
He says.
I'm shattering their lives
Making them miserable.
But I can't stop, I don't know how
and they won't stop me.
He was the only one who saw the truth about me
I play the victim
I'm pathetic.
They're all afraid to hurt my feelings.
He's not the bad guy
I trapped him
Now everyone else has to deal with me.
And then my best friend looks me in the eye
With more intensity, more sensitivity than I can handle anymore
And she says,
"You're not broken.
You're not a ruin.
You are not to blame."
My blood sings with the love, this undeserved love
And she hears me, hears the thought before I can say it
And cuts in,
"You deserve love. We love to love you.
You are not too much."

Leaking
Dripping
How is this happening?
I fixed the cracks
I'm ice cold
But that is me on the floor
Puddling
Pooling
In the glow of kindness
The tenderness will kill me

Glimmers in a Corporate Girl Weekend

Fresh air whooshing past me as I leave the office. The glow from the text that reads, "we still on for tonight?" The slick gloss sliding across my lips. The drumbeat of my favorite getting-ready song. The sweet scent of lotion gliding over my legs and arms. Light catching in the shimmer on my eyelids. The tart citrus in my cocktail. The strong belting notes from the singer of the live band. Warm air freeing me of my jacket. The edge of the bar digging into my hip as I lean in to order more tequila, giggling. The burn of the shot as it makes its way down my throat. The trickle of a smile from my lips, thanking him for paying. A brush of fingers on mine and the way the space starts to wobble, everything becoming louder, funnier. Yelling secrets that should be whispered–the music is so loud, so perfectly loud I can feel it in my ribcage. The warm, salty late night french fries and corn dogs. Waking up in my pulsing room with a frantic heartbeat. The dripping yolks of eggs in my breakfast sandwich, served at a table underneath a vent blowing cold air on my neck. Faintly pressing on the bruise found on my hip, speculating when in the night it appeared.

I press in, begging myself to pull away
Hope lives in my lungs,
Expanding me with air
Terror sucks up each breath
I'm lifting off the ground
I'm digging my grave

I claw at the hands that cling to him
My fingers bleed
My throat is raw
From screaming to not give anything away
But I'm singing like a canary
Screeching like a hawk

I'm melting in the sunlight
And basking in it
Trying to scoop the remains of myself into a safe place
So I don't drip through the cracks of the sidewalk
While embracing the heat of the pavement

A smile I can feel all the way down to my toes
Every brush of fingertips makes me glow
He's the heat of a spotlight on the stage I stand on
Lighting me up and letting me shine
I feel like a star

Backstage

I pace in my all-black clothes,
Nervously wondering - will they like it?
Will I do this right?
Am I needed?
Three weeks later,
I take a glass from her hand,
While she flees to slip on a new gown –
I hand him his shoes, I zip her dress,
I kiss a teary cheek
Because tonight we say goodbye
To this dance we have created together

I ask him if he's ever been in love
Because I'm dying to know every detail of him.
When he asks me back,
I don't know the answer.
Surely I was
But I don't know anymore.
And now...
I feel like I am in love
When I'm laughing with my sister until we're sobbing, howling.
I feel in love
When my best friend texts me to make sure I made it home safely.
I feel in love
When I'm singing karaoke with the whole bar
When my answer is right at trivia
With the green tint on everything after a summer storm
With every 30-something learning a new language so they can travel
With the lime shoved into a beer bottle
With the weeds that push up through the cracks of the cement,
Determined to live
I want to romance the cool breeze in early October
I want to linger like the mint in his toothpaste
Or the sound from a struck piano key in an empty room
I am absorbing the beams of sunlight through leaves
I am diving into a pool of starlight
I am in love with everything
In love, in love, in love
Am I?

How it Feels to be a lovergirl

My long, almond-shaped nails
Sink into my skin
I feel the piercing of each layer
As I dig in further, further
As my warm blood
Begins to ooze down my chest
I peel my skin back
Exposing my ribs
Viscera makes my hands sticky
And I drag my claws down
Until my guts fall to my feet
People pass me by,
A glance, a grimace
I reach back in and crack my ribs
One by one
Bone marrow spatters my face
I finally feel my beating heart
Spurting blood with each pump
I take it gingerly, so gently
Hold it above my head
And wait

Hot breaths mingle, humid and sweet
His hands skim my ribs
And we are skimming across the surface of a deeper lake
I see the friendly weeds underneath,
Reaching, inviting us in
We will dive under soon
Soon we will plunge
Into the warm, embracing water
But for now
We skip like stones

The word Love rolls around in my head like a marble
I feel every letter, round and smooth,
Open and vulnerable
Sometimes it threatens to spring out of my mouth
Like a pinball
After a press of a hand, or a gentle smile
I enjoy the honey of it in a kiss
I smell it on his neck, clean and earthy

What if it does escape,
And what if the glass shatters
When I expose it to cold air,
Becoming jagged and sharp,
Shards scattered between us
An obstacle to avoid
As I try to step toward him?

One day it might jump out
To sweeten or spoil
But until then
I hold the word under my tongue
I let it etch deep grooves in my brain
Whirring like a fan
And tickling the back of my throat

He cocks an eyebrow
and I know, I just know
He's adding to the pile

The pile of reasons
He doesn't like me anymore
Shoved into a corner of his brain

He'll scoop it all up
In a few months' time
Realizing how much there is

And then he'll hand me a bag full of them
and tell me we're done
And my heart will break

Every stupid comment
Every forgotten errand
Every boring story

Every favor done for me
Every meal cooked for me
Every drink bought for me

Each one goes in the pile
The evidence that I deserve
The inevitable sorrow that will come

I can feel the soft velvet
Of the bag he'll put them in
Feel the sagging of my shoulders
Under the weight of it

He will carry the bag to my car for me
Tell me he didn't realize until now
How many reasons there were
Close the door as gently as he can

So I tell my friends
Not to hold their breath for me
I'm irrepressibly happy now
But will be shattered soon

Soon I will cry on their couches
Dissolve in my bathtub
Drown myself in their embraces
Beg for their kindness

"Enjoy it,"
My therapist
My best friend
My sister all say

"Don't let your past
Wreck your present
Don't let one bad apple
Spoil your whole life"

And they are right
And I am angry
Gritting my teeth
Against brittle memory

Do you know how unfair it feels
To know I didn't deserve mistreatment
I didn't earn unkindness
But I still put stock in it

To feel this kind of gratitude
For every kind word
Because surely
It's undeserved

Not to be dramatic,
But my name on your lips is my favorite song
I'm trying not to be too much
When I tell you I can't get enough of you
I'm not overstating
When I say that your laugh sends sparks through me
That every brush of your fingertips
On my back
Through my hair
Feels like fiber optics
Lighting up every vein, every capillary in my body
I'm trying not to run you off
With my enthusiasm
I don't want to freak you out
By going too fast, too hard
But if people are made for each other
It feels like you were made for me
Healing wounds you don't see
Setting me free in ways
I didn't know I needed to be
I'll expose myself and tell you
I'm scared of scaring you
When I say
I like, I want, I see,
I need, I feel, I l–
I lo–
I love
I love
I love you

I've always had a hard time with favorites
How am I supposed to choose one thing to love the most
When I love the things I do for different reasons?
I love pink because it reminds me of Valentines
But I love to wear the color blue
My favorite scent at home is citrus
But my favorite candle is eucalyptus
Suddenly, coney dogs are my favorite food
Detroit is my favorite place
Your eyes are my favorite color
I want to go every place you do
With a certainty so strong it scares me
You can have all my favorites
If I get to have you

The Girls' Room

Oh my god you are so beautiful!
I love your top
I have those shoes at home!
I have a tampon, do you need one?
Here, can I fix your tag for you?
Look, we match!
Wait, what are you drinking?
Someone left their phone in here!
Oh my gosh I live right near there!
We should meet up
I'll talk to him for you!
He's so sweet
So yummy, want to try?
Ew, we hate him
I can walk with you if you want
Does anyone have eyelash glue?
There's no paper towels in that one
Where did you get that necklace?
I'll send you the link
Here try my lip gloss
Let's exchange numbers
Let's see each other again
I love you!

I'm talking behind your back
Every chance I get
I'm whispering "i love you"
Over your shoulder
Underwater
In front of your closed eyes
i love you
I draw it on your back
I tap it on your thigh
I squeeze your hand three times
i love you
Hoping that you'll feel it
Because it's quietly seeping
From every pore of me

Kallie

She is a flurry of words
A burst of sparks
Stories pour out of her
Like a popped bottle of champagne
She can't help but make art
Stumbling into poignancy
In every phrase she speaks
You suddenly believe in yourself
With how fiercely she believes in you
Recklessly supportive
Endlessly generous
Connecting every dot she sees
In the maddening, beautiful,
Wonderful, complicated
Experience of being a person
Turning life into art
Every smile, every tear, every curse
Made beautiful in her hands

My whole life I've considered myself profoundly unlucky.
It's a joke that covers my whole family.
I'm not a winning type:
Not getting an upgrade on a flight,
Or a free coffee,
Or finding a dollar on the street.
It's just been part of my life -
Something to step around
As I try to make my way in the world.

But today
I spent my day in the perfect sunshine
I laughed with my family,
Kissing their cheeks before they drove home.
I go to bed with you
I feel your warmth radiating through me
I dream of the sun on your skin
The way your shoulders shake when you laugh
I live a life I couldn't have dreamed for myself
And I wonder
How I became the luckiest person on earth

Dayle

An optimist and a realist
A practical dreamer
A fairytale creature who will help me fix my real world

You remind me that life is silly
You make every ugly thing beautiful
You can the potential in everything

With a coat of paint, or a lighthearted laugh
The old dresser, the bully, the bad day
Turn beautiful

Tell me how to do it like you -
I can't see it before you show me
Before your magic touch turns everything golden

Shaking with fear I turn to you
"Don't worry, we'll fix it," you say
And we do

"No you are not stupid,"
"Yes you can come over,"
"Don't take it seriously,"

And the sun shines and we lay on your couch draped in blankets
    with a buffet of snacks
I cry, laughing until it hurts, and life is so bright and beautiful
    that I have to shade my eyes

Oh my god the thrill I get
When we walk out the door
We are parting for our workdays
And I get a kiss, "love you, drive safe"
Am I glowing?
I can't stop smiling
Can everyone see it?
When we walk through the grocery store
He holds our basket
Hand on my back
Can't they all see how I'm sparkling?
I feel like starlight
It's glinting in my eyes
Particles falling off the tips of my hair
All of our day to day routines
Absolute bliss
How can he sleep at night
When I'm lit up like a whole sky?

I'm out of poems to write!
You have taken all the creativity from me
Because there's no excitement in feeling so safe
It's the emotional equivalent
Of eating tomato soup and grilled cheese
Warm and joyful and nourishing
I stand on the summit of a mountain
Drinking in the fresh, fresh air
Protected from the cold
In the jacket you wore in case I needed it
The sun beams on my face
Blushing my cheeks
Chapping my grinning lips
Absorbing all this contentment like vitamin D
I'm driving down a country road, slowly,
On a warm Spring day
And there's no pollen
And the windows are down
And there's nothing artistic in stability
How do you write about being at peace?
There is no sorrow in this comfort
But I will scrape the bowl
Drink in the air
And bask in the sunshine
Because I have never been happier

Thank You

Sarah Brackett, you were the first person to encourage me to write. This is the result of that. Thank you to every person who heard me timidly (or drunkenly) admit that I was writing a little bit and thought maybe I'd publish something and said "yes." Thank you to every friend who held my hand and saw my tears and listened to every ugly thing I had to say. Alex, I could not have dreamed up a better best friend. My siblings – my heart beats for you. Mom, Dad – you didn't hesitate to hoist me up when I held up my hands and cried for you. Chris… I'll keep it simple for obvious reasons… I love you. I could never hope to express my love in words. I am, without a doubt, the luckiest girl in the world.

About the Author

Halley lives in Atlanta with her beau, a beautiful baby puppygirl, and her most beloved familiar and piece of her soul, her kitty BBG. She never meant to be a writer and may never be again, but you can find her on Instagram at @hookedbyhalley.

www.ingramcontent.com/pod-product-compliance
Lightning Source LLC
Chambersburg PA
CBHW072035150726

47999CB00002B/921